# A Spotter's Guide
# To Invisible Things

Writing in her second language, **Laura Theis** received a Distinction from Oxford University's MSt in Creative Writing. Her work appears in journals such as *Poetry*, *Mslexia*, *Magma*, *Rattle*, and *Strange Horizons*, and anthologies by Candlestick Press, Broken Sleep Books, Pan Macmillan, and Aesthetica, amongst many others. Her Elgin-Award-nominated debut *'how to extricate yourself'*, an Oxford Poetry Library Book-of-the-Month, won the Brian Dempsey Memorial Prize. She was the recipient of the Society of Authors' Arthur Welton Award, the AM Heath Prize, EAL Oxford Brookes Poetry Prize, Mogford Prize, Hammond House International Literary Award, the Alpine Fellowship and a Forward Prize nomination. A runner-up for the Mairtin Crawford Award, she was shortlisted for the Women Poets' Prize, the Bridport Prize, the Margaret Reid Poetry Prize, the Hippocrates Prize and a finalist for numerous other literary awards including the National Poetry Competition and the BBC Short Story Award.

# Contents

Acknowledgements                                                          6


**Chapter One:**
**A Spotter's Guide to Roots & Riddles**                                  8

miðnæturblár                                                              9
Six Things Taygete Had To Learn Without Being Taught                     10
in my mother tongue the name for grand piano is wing                     12
supernatural                                                             13
a poem in which I use the word 'betoken' for the first time in my life   15
for a spell                                                              15
water bucket                                                             17
the day I became a native speaker                                        18
Ameisenverteilungsmaschine                                              20
The Tree Comes Inside                                                    21
the cuteness workshop                                                    22
birch / star / sister                                                    23
the silent sea                                                           24
This Poem Will Never Become A Multi-Million Dollar Netflix Series        26
The Selkies Visit At Bath Time                                           27
Tell Us About Yourself                                                   28


**Chapter Two:**
**Bindweed for Beginners**                                               29

the nursery                                                              30
ode to june                                                              31
I went on a walk without my phone                                        32
in which we introduce ourselves                                          34
Walpurgis Eve                                                            36
a walk past the rooftops                                                 37
Jazz                                                                     38
I will miss even the bindweed                                            39

packing advice for the one who is leaving .......... 40
a sci-fi story about flying urn hauntings that would make
    an excellent Hollywood blockbuster .......... 41
what you meant when you promised we'd go to the circus .......... 42
furnishings .......... 43
after matching with the sky on various dating apps .......... 44
Passer .......... 46
proof if proof were needed .......... 47
the dream house .......... 48
dwelling in a warm place .......... 50
Advice from an Alligator Pear .......... 52
frog .......... 54

**Chapter Three:**
**A Spotter's Guide to Wings & Wonder**     **55**

Sleep Lessons from Birds .......... 56
this is when .......... 57
22 02 2022 .......... 58
Once There Were Willows .......... 59
Eyrar .......... 60
animal rescue .......... 62
taming a night mare in ten easy steps .......... 63
Surgeon .......... 66
I went out today looking for wonder .......... 67
We Weren't Raised by Wolves But .......... 68

**Thank-Yous**     **69**

# Acknowledgements

This book owes its existence to the generosity of the 2022 *Arthur Welton Award* by the Society of Authors, and to Rebecca Goss and Helen Eastman. With everlasting gratitude to them and also to the editors and judges of the following publications and prizes:

'Ameisenverteilungsmaschine' and 'miðnæturblár' with gratitude to *POETRY* and the *Women Poets' Prize* funded by the Rebecca Swift Foundation.

'a poem in which I use the word 'betoken' for the first time in my life' with gratitude to the EAL *Oxford Brookes Poetry Prize,* Will Harris, and Oxford Brookes Poetry for the *Forward Prize* nomination.

'a sci-fi story about flying urn hauntings that would make an excellent Hollywood blockbuster' with gratitude to *Coastal Shelf.*

'Dwelling in a warm place' with gratitude to *Magma* and Alycia Pirmohamed.

'Eyrar' with gratitude to the 2022 *Live Canon Anthology.*

'For a spell' with gratitude to *The Phare,* the *WriteWords Poetry Prize* and the *Mairtin Crawford Poetry Prize.*

'Frog' with gratitude to *The Friday Poem.*

'Furnishings' with gratitude to *Poetry Is Not Dead* (Dempsey & Windle).

'in my mother tongue the name for grand piano is wing' with gratitude to Fiona Benson, David Constantine, Rachel Long and the 2022 *National Poetry Competition* and Philip Gross and the 2023 *Poets and Players Competition.*

'I went on a walk without my phone' with gratitude to the 2021 *Anthology Poetry Prize.*

'I went out today looking for wonder' with gratitude to Candlestick Press, Jo Bell, the *Winchester Poetry Prize Anthology,* and the *Spelt Poetry Prize.*

'I will miss even the bindweed' with gratitude to Michèle Mendelssohn and *No Place Like Home* (Pan Macmillan).

'ode to june' with gratitude to Candlestick Press.

'Six Things Taygete Had To Learn Without Being Taught' with gratitude to Live Canon, the *Aesthetica Creative Writing Award*, the *Mairtin Crawford Poetry Prize*, the *Tom Howard/Margaret Reid Poetry Contest*, the *Acumen Poetry Prize*, and the *Women Poets' Prize*, funded by the Rebecca Swift Foundation.

'Sleep Lessons From Birds' with gratitude to *whiptail* and *Obheal's Five-Words Prize*.

'Supernatural' with gratitude to *Rattle* and Susy Kamber.

'Tell Us About Yourself' with gratitude to *Last Stanza*.

'The Silent Sea', 'the dream house' and 'packing advice for the one who is leaving' with gratitude to *Sylvia Magazine*.

'The nursery', 'in which we introduce ourselves', 'dwelling in a warm place', 'birch / star / sister', 'The Tree Comes Inside', 'Six Things Taygete Had To Learn Without Being Taught' and 'We Weren't Raised by Wolves But' with gratitude to Katherine Rundell, John Burnside, Gillian Clark, and the *Alpine Fellowship Writing Prize*.

'This is when' with gratitude to Glyn Maxwell and the *AUB Poetry Award Anthology*.

'water bucket' with gratitude to *Horses of a different colour* (Dempsey & Windle) and the *Brian Dempsey Memorial Prize*.

'Walpurgis Eve' with gratitude to *Worlds of Possibility*.

'What you meant when you promised we'd go to the circus' with gratitude to Ó Bhéal's *Five Words Vol XIV*.

# Chapter One

## A Spotter's Guide
## to Roots and Riddles

## miðnæturblár

we have to look up when we search
for our dead

even though we buried them
in the ground

but the dead like to call to
us from the moon

they try to spell out their wildering
words in clouds or meteors

they try to wave at us
through murmurations

and other such avian patterns
in significant moments

they do this to teach us
to make lifting

up our eyes a habit
*remember* they say *once*

*every day for*
*a couple of minutes*

*the entire sky turns*
*your favourite colour:*

*the very darkest*
*shade of blue*

# Six Things Taygete Had To Learn Without Being Taught

I. how to scream

as a doe you have
no voice to speak of

but you can still make a soft
snorting noise when alarmed

you may even still sing
when in love

a kazoo rasp crossed with a rusty screen
door in the wind

II. how to be beautiful while unconscious

don't
it isn't
safe

III.  how to be a moon

be fallow
elusive

but as sharp as a
shard of a god's heart

know the meaning
of fawning

make sure you aren't
followed

*here and then here*
*and then gone*

IV. how to rest

fold all four legs into a nest of moss
under the hazel branches

or slow dance along the night
sky with your sisters

learn what you can
from the comets

anyone who knows what it means to be hounded
knows how to be a star


V. how to hunt and be hunted at the same time

the stars understand
it's never easy to tell the prey from the goddess

the goddess
advises

you need to be fast
you need to be less

of yourself than everyone else
only this will help you be quicker

    a)   on your feet
    b)   than him and his lightning

ask all six
of your sisters

remember the wisdom
of comets

*here and then here*
*and then gone*

# in my mother tongue the name for grand piano is wing

in my mother tongue
words can be feathered

which turns them into
old jokes or proverbs

owning a bird
in my mother tongue

is a sign of great madness:
you can accuse someone

with an outrageous opinion
of cheeping and chirping

if you want to convey
that you are flabbergasted or awed

in my mother tongue
you might say: *my dear swan*

which is what I think
when I first hear you play

as your fingers move over
the keys I wonder

what gets lost in translation
between music and birdsong

whether both soar above
our need to shift between words

then I remember
in my mother tongue

the name for grand piano
is wing

## supernatural

mist is water

      without surface

         and yet it will not


         only swallow the past but

     bring it up again too

if it feels in the mood


let me tell you how

     it steps through the vapour

          towards you now


        not like a twin trapped

     in a mirror reaching both hands

towards you through the glass


or a pinniped

     coming up for air

from the unsounded deep


not like a sleeper breaking

through a dream's stillness

into the clang and dry of the waking


no it emerges

composed and unhurried

moving backwards like a riddle


a girl wearing not so much

a dress as a violent

blaze of chenille


determined to make you

say that you now

believe in ghosts

## a poem in which I use the word 'betoken' for the first time in my life

here's a little bauble of dust for you
to hit me with: hard

so I go down then get up and
hug you like a monkey catcher

I blow up dripped in blood then get up once more
dipped in honey

the hug entails all the gratitude of a grave and
all the gravity of a fleeing mare: look

you have made a mark that betokens
the death of light

## for a spell

the solitude is
an unexpected present

it's a hot day
the river bank's earth cakes and ridges

I bake along with it then swim
in the dirty dirty river

I share the water with things that float
bird feathers bottles blossoms

condoms and copulating
dragonflies

I share the river with things which pollute
blaring engines and motor oil

the bridge ahead bears strange graffiti I turn away
swim back towards the towel I stole

from the dog and a waiting
tupperware full of cherries

maybe this is what you meant
when you wrote that

it's moments like these we stay
alive for

the water phasing into
a thin layer of warmth over the cold undercurrent

I am afraid of happiness
but floating here

in this stream of water and diluted sewage
I let it in

## water bucket

we can tell it is fairy water by the way
it appears and disappears
inside the bucket

it might be a gift or a carelessness
some mysteries are best left
unexamined

however only
the hopeless
children know that

if you drink from it a certain way
it can turn you invisible
in parts

if you use it to drench
your shoes with a knack
you can use them to walk

on the river's surface
for up to an hour like some
once-great men in a book

a drop of it inside your
water spray bottle
can will the willow

to murmur or unbloom
a bindweed trumpet
even the ghost-white

wilted lilies could
(but should not)
be revived

## the day I became a native speaker

I am ashamed
to admit it

but when the body crashed
through my skylight in a fury of glass and rain

my first thought
was not concern for the person and whether

they had survived
their horrendous fall

my first thought was oh fuck me
how am I supposed to afford to repair this

my first impulse was to run downstairs to get
some towels to catch the downpour

before it soaked through my entire bed
to get a broom and get rid of the sharp shards

on my pillow
l had to make a conscious effort to turn

my attention instead
to the victim of the accident

crumpled on the floor next to the bed
and wearing some sort of feathery coat

when they stood
they were too tall for my slanted ceiling

and had to crouch under the roof
to unfold their wet tangled garment

into what I now realised
were wings

soaked through from the rain
but miraculously uninjured

and my mind went oh
oh

then it went almost blank
forgot all about the damage and skylight

the rain still pelting down on my duvet
I had fallen in love because I am like that

shallow and easily swayed by beauty
I did not say what is all this

and who are you and why are you here
instead I said what people in this country

always say in fraught situations
I said *I'll put the kettle on, shall I?*

## Ameisenverteilungsmaschine

my mother tells me
nobody wants to read poems about
ant distribution machines
in fact nobody wants to read poems at all
they are unnecessary

no one has ever heard of such a thing as a wealthy poet
so it isn't really worthwhile she tells me I should consider writing
a best-selling novel or maybe the screenplay for a family saga
if I insist on being difficult
at least give the short story collection a go

except she says all of this in German
and the German word for ant distribution machine is
Ameisenverteilungsmaschine
I decide it is now my favourite word I decide to write the poem
to be poor and obscure

it will be a poem of defiance
about what at first seems like a nonsense invention
who would buy such a useless machine
who needs help distributing ants
they are not very popular pets

but here's the beauty of my Ameisenverteilungsmaschine
it actually turns the critters into lovely new shapes
tiny giraffes little kangaroos and cows
a miniature camel small enough to make it
through the ear of a largeish needle

# The Tree Comes Inside

behind the opaque
kitchen window
waits the darkness
of the night-time garden

I look but
for once I don't see
my own reflection
in the glass

all I see
is a tree trying
to root into the kitchen floor
cracking the tiles open with the effort

and all of a sudden
I am standing
tall in the night garden air
surrendering to my own growth

sap rises up
to fix the wound
on my bleeding knee
I feel

for a moment
what it is like to breathe
to know time only in seasons
and recovery

to know nothing
of minutes
or judgement
or shame

inside the tree looks on
in new-found surprise
as her branches turn into
my clueless hands

# the cuteness workshop

I never knew people could
have such heated opinions on the subject
of cuteness

but when Isabel tells us to share stories of
cute objects in our possession
most of us admit to a deep-seated unease

the woman next to me extracts a small
flute-playing porcelain angel from her coat pocket
spins it around frowning with undisguised disgust

*my mother-in-law gave this to me*
*when I married her son so*
*it was clear I had to keep it because it was*

*her approval but both my husband and his mother*
*are dead now I will have to hold on to it forever*
*at least until I -* she falls silent

I am close enough to catch the offending musician's
expression of soundless saccharine menace
I can almost hear him hiss his retort

*I never asked to be this red-cheeked and round*
*I certainly never wanted to be so small as to fit*
*into somebody's loveless palm*

# birch / star / sister

first: a birch
her branches apply themselves
splitting the fresh air
now it is quieter than only a moment ago
the sun broils in the verdure
we live in this heat now
we look away as we pass the burning trees

later: a star and her siblings
how slowly they float
didn't we use to have highways for the stars to go fast?
my sister comes up with new rubbish like this all the time
it is galling now
why are you the sole other skin
in this forest that blurs and heats our trees?

men who had hands
have long traded them in
for red branches
rivers too
of course we ought to say nothing
passing beneath the stars or
the legs of the hanged

## the silent sea

it is not perhaps
our greatest crime

hardly worth mentioning amongst
all the heinous acts of pollution

oil spills and melting
ice caps but

we have also stolen the silence
from under the waves


the whales that live here cannot
recall a life without the constant

drone of cruise ship motors
which have turned their ocean

into the kind of noise box
familiar to anyone

who ever tried to have
a conversation in a crowded nightclub


there's no room for nuance
when communication means

someone shouting something
over a background din

knowing that whether or not
they will be understood

is left up to the guesswork
of lip reading


these past months of sudden quiet
marked the first time the whales

were granted the bliss
of real stillness

their listening
laced with wonder


scientists believe their language
will change now

hydrophones have been installed
to pick up the altered

songs born from silence
allowing for new complexity


their first poetry

## This Poem Will Never Become A Multi-Million Dollar Netflix Series

Starlings are dancing a slow
orderly ceilidh in my drainpipe.

I peer up at them and see their
dotted underbellies shuffling past.

Every so often a bird
poo flies by my window.

Festivities concluded, they leave
in a string of winged exuberance.

Meanwhile, a birch is losing copper
coins in the neighbour's garden.

I will not hit my word count today.
I've not written a single sentence.

An ancient acorn is growing
white roots in a water jar.

## The Selkies Visit At Bath Time

it is the only moment in my day that I am
not lonely or in pain

the heat of the bath water eviscerates all of my
aging body's aches and complaints

around me the selkies' half-human
company soothes my solitary soul

their presence is a gift I refuse to question
their song is not beautiful

their chatter not all that friendly
they give me quizzical glances

they say things like
*did you know that in seal years*

*you would most likely already be dead?*
but in that they feel almost like family

and their animal eyes are soulful and deep
and uncannily familiar too:

I was given a stuffed white seal pup at birth
it shared my name and my life

across oceans and contracting years
and grew greyer and more beloved

the only childhood relic that
I have not lost or had to give up

perhaps the reason the bath selkies visit
is pity that we failed to truly turn into each other

because she was a toy and I was a child
who had yet to learn I deserved magic

## Tell Us About Yourself

no I don't want to present
my life to you instead I want to give myself
over to the people

who found a single dinosaur bone and
made it into a dragon with powers of fire and flight
and an agenda involving abductions and gold

the people who saw a pale round
in the night sky and brought it alive
as a goddess

who witnessed summer
rain and invented the sadness
of seraphim

I want them to find some of my old scraps
of paper my favourite moth-eaten jumper
my wisdom tooth

the four plants I killed
and the one I kept alive
and make a fiction of me

Chapter Two

**Bindweed for Beginners**

## the nursery

it seems that he wants us
alive but disconnected

from a seedling we are
living by ourselves

each of us forlornly growing
in our individual pots

we are overfed de-liced and
richly watered but

in the wild our roots would reach
for one another and amalgamate

we'd share our nutrients
and knowledge

if we sensed danger we would pulse
a parlous warning to each other

but it turns out the distance
is too great even for that

as he carries us away
towards an unknown fate

# ode to june

mountains! forgive me
I wasn't made for climbing you
for I am a creature of leisure

goals! forgive me
I have only one:
to eat like a spoiled bird or

the child of a fairy
nothing but bowls upon bowls
of fresh cherries

see I am a creature of pleasure
of soft pyjamas and languid reading and wild
river swimming and strawberry seeking and

fireside singing
forgive me ambition
forgive me competition

I am not in the market for winning
I am a joy-hungry
recreationing summer fiend

a cross between pool float and pillow
come find me ambling in the meadow
spot me swanning through the twilight

here am I and here's my glee
and here are the red-branched dogwoods
the caraganas and willows

# I went on a walk without my phone

I went on a walk without
my phone

its absence was
a lightness in my pocket

I saw the fractal infinity
of cherry blossoms

and the cheerful beauty
of the season's last bluebells

but I did not take
a picture of them

to filter and edit and upload
at a later time

there were no little pings
to distract me

no urgent messages from friends
that needed consoling

my thoughts settled
on me like falling petals

why have I lived my recent years
outside of myself

attuned to the chaos-drunk world in my hand
and not the soft easeful one at my feet?

with no headphones in my ears
I sat down on the dappled grass

and let the birdsong
wash over me

a fluting of information
in an incomprehensible language

I did not know what time it was but I felt close
to understanding

what my time was
and what it could be

for a couple of unscreened minutes
I was the freest creature in the world

## in which we introduce ourselves

everyone cares about
the lonely whale bull

we believe him to be sad
singing on his own for

nobody's benefit
we identify with his perceived

pointlessness what good is a whale
without his pod

we wonder


& we all care about cliff hangers
if the film opens with a shot

of a climber dangling
from a precipice

we don't want the stranger to fail
or come to harm

we want to shout something
loud and trite like

hang on in there buddy


& we are primed for the colour red
because it might spell somebody's blood

we are programmed to draw
close to each other at night

around whatever passes for a fire
to share whatever passes for a story

whilst each of us breathes through
eight hundred trees' worth of oxygen

which is why when we pray we pray mostly to wood

## Walpurgis Eve

Each year, come Walpurgis,
Father bolts the gates

at sunset, double-locks
the front door.

He does this, he says
to keep looters and pranksters away

hold mischief and revels
at bay, shut out the mutinous night.

This year, Walpurgis Eve came
with a gale force. But Father

now used to dismissing
everything wild in the air

or the eyes of young girls
never bothered to hide

the key to the cabinet under the stairs
where the maid keeps mop bucket and broom.

And so I went with my sisters,
I'm here with my sisters

I went with my sisters
to dance.

## a walk past the rooftops

I am lost
to the sadness of the gods
those dear jesters
who aren't used to
denying or restricting themselves

whose skull-like heads
might throw up on
any one of us
at any minute

on a corroding bridge over
an undecided river
beneath the stony glow
of a vanity moon
I am lost

to this dolorous city
hidden high above the night sky
gifted but useless the gods
continue their endless forging and forging of nebulas

foxes flicker in dark corners
like dogs that only belong
to themselves
one shares a sorrow
with the street lamps

life is
pelting past
like
invisible
rain

the night has teeth
the night is where
good things go
to avoid getting discovered

# Jazz

the thing is we can
hear it everywhere now

in the swing of the sun's arc
from day into night

the blue notes of the wind
in our autumn trees

there's a pinch of it in the call and response
of the orca pods out in the strait

it's in the polyrhythms of our
unreleased hopes

the complex chords of our
november grief

it is right here, now,
in this improvised silence

waiting for your voice

# I will miss even the bindweed

I will miss even the bindweed
that strangles my apple trees
with its insidious tendrils
even the nettles and brambles

I will miss the creaking stairs
these particular birds and
this particular angle of the moon
the lovelorn fox cat screaming at night like a changeling

the cracked ceiling and the slow-sinking
walls that sometimes decide
to drop a framed picture
the way an unruly horse bucks its rider

I will miss the scorching tap
the constant drip of minor emergencies
like that time when there was water
running out of the kitchen ceiling lamps

or when the key broke in the lock
and the landlord cat-burglared through a smashed window
into the overladen cupboard under the stairs
where the rats once found all our spaghetti

I will miss every single floorboard
the broken oven that burnt all my cakes
the dirty windows
I will miss the boring road and the overfamiliar walk

I will miss the years of my life
that I was kept safe behind these doors
I will miss being known well by a house
and who I was when I lived here

## Packing advice for the one who is leaving

Not the razor nor the stars -
never the stars. Your proximity
should be a window but not
as wondrous as a very red apple.

Never torches
beneath the porous night roof.
But food for the little one's unicorn.
But the lazy sighs of emergency mushrooms.

Goodbyes should be sweet storms.
Start learning in the school of night and quiet.
Never sleep in the same bed twice. Remember:
Sadness does not make for a good ladder.

## sci-fi story about flying urn hauntings that would make an excellent Hollywood blockbuster

I think you should write the poem at about three
or four am when you're overly tired and the thin
fabric that masks your insanity in the daytime
has been torn aside

the dog should be curled up to next to you
like a small smelly shadow on the indigo sofa
you rent from a woman called
something like Charlotte

who is into maths-related dirty talk
and likes to say things like *in order for a*
*function to have a left inverse it must*
*be injective* to her lover on the phone

also I think the poem should be about
that idea you know the one
the sci-fi story about the haunting urns
where after your death you get to fly

around in a little amphora steered by your own
uploaded consciousness to spook
and annoy your surviving family members
and how that says something about what kind

of a fun future we could have looked forward to
if humanity hadn't opted to not have a future at all
I think tomorrow you could force Charlotte to listen
to you recite the poem in your special poetry voice

as revenge for all the overheard dirty maths you have to
suffer through and then someone should buy the film
rights to the idea so that for once in your life you and the dog
would have enough money to get a place with a sofa you could

rent out to a skint neurotic poet-insomniac of your own

# what you meant when you promised we'd go to the circus

the spotlight is a pinprick
of sun through the blinds the lion

is a calico kitten asleep on the
windowsill the trapeze

is an empty bag slung over the back
of a chair the dancers are all

specks of silvery dust
the sad clown is me

spilling half of my coffee onto my
whitest dress because my hands are shaking

the magic trick is the lover
performing a very arcane

disappearing act

# furnishings

once again the small god and I
find ourselves
at war

we disagree of course about many things
but most often and most violently
about the purpose of rugs

for my sins I believe they ought to be
flat uncreased surfaces
splayed out parallel to the floor

whereas the small god is convinced
they need to be bunched up beveled twisted and pummeled
into complicated three-dimensional objets d'art

we can't help ourselves
we have to undo each other's efforts
several times a day with increasing urgency

the small god forever
bunching and punching and rearranging
with teeth paws and huffs of annoyance

and me on my hands and knees
straightening and flattening
with the air of a put-upon dowager's maid

it's a strange compulsion on both our parts
a frustrating lesson in perpetual futility
perhaps as close to purgatory

as we can ever get this side of the veil
we pretend not to know
this is just another shape

that love takes
furnishing the small space
between heaven and hell

# after matching with the sky on various dating apps

someone who provides their own
halo does not need my admiration

it's not that I don't believe in the sky
I was just never big on weather

to some the sky is just a joke
or something to protest against

clouded over or uncovered it still displays
an obscure anatomy of violence

even night skies or red ones
even trickster weather holding birds and whirlwinds

it's all just not that impressive to me
if I am one of those glib nay-sayers

it's not fear or courage
I've just never felt that casadastraphobic pull

ok yes it sure is a nice
backdrop for running horses

somewhere for darkness
to retreat to

a fire receptacle
the singing echo of ozone

and for some it's medicine
sustenance on a bleak weekday

and yeah granted the aurora is so wild it's almost edible
but does the sky have a sky of its own

is it jealous of all the action the rain gets
why are we talking as if the sky

were a stranger and not
the most beautiful bellend in the world

here's the deal, sky, I do not bow to the absurdity of your
perfection your wetness thunder nervy lightning

I've jokingly nicknamed you
the earth's idiot cousin

you know you'll have to work a little harder
to get me out of the house

## Passer

I too had a great love once.
I only met him a single time
for perhaps seven minutes.

Lying under a fig tree by the sea
enchanted by blues and wavesong
I spotted his round feathered shape

through the canopy, devouring
a dark fig while hanging upside down
like a Tuscan gecko and suddenly felt

a kinship so great I recognised him
as a shard of my bones,
unseparated.

His friends all headed towards the ocean
but he waited a moment longer, eying me,
puffed up in his own glorious softness.

Then he flew off.
And I was still whole.
It was love.

## proof if proof were needed

that transformation can be effortless
when we became the music
moving through time like a liquid

we were bright birds resisting the sky
exulting in our luminous bodies our salt
coloured plumage our wings of muscle and sinew

in every dimension of movement
we were verse made manifest were grace
beyond gender or stage

we ended by bowing to you and like in each movement
there was a message for you in this too
the same one every unremarkable dove

has been trying to convey to you since your childhood

*you were right*
*all along*
*another*
*world*
*is*
*possible*

# the dream house

at first no one noticed anything strange
about her language
when she talked about the house

*I've fallen in love with the place*
she would say *it was love at first sight*
*I am completely obsessed with it*

people just smiled and let her go on about its dual
aspect bedrooms and how it boasted
a moulded architrave cornice

and segmental pediment a flagstone fireplace flanked by
Doric pilasters with window seats shutters and easy-to-vacuum
polished teak floorboards

but by the time she reached the carved oak cantilevered
staircase providing a dramatic centrepiece with sturdy balusters
and thick square newels

their smiles would waver a little
and they'd have to think of polite ways
to escape from the conversation

by then her eyes would have glazed over slightly as she explained
about the massive stone arch
which carries the weight of the central chimney stack

grabbing her interlocutor's arm she would urgently whisper
that the driveway is approached
through honey-coloured gate piers

her cheeks flushing pink at the thought of the sunken
lawn bordered by ground-covering plants to the front of the house
a south facing herbaceous border with a wide variety of perennials and evergreens

with tears in her eyes she'd reveal that beyond the kitchen garden's yew
        hedging there was nothing
but the quiet of a delightful spinney which adjoins open countryside bounded
only by a long-winded brook

that a stone pillared veranda
provides shelter on drizzly days
that she had thought love was a delusion until she found the one

## dwelling in a warm place

nothing heats
as well as shame

burning your cheeks
from the inside

is there something
you did to deserve

this life of a spoiled beloved
heifer?

storm, urn or warm tongue?
let me guess

which of the three
will it be for you?

on rough winter evenings
they sometimes scratch

at the edge of your conscience
the so-called less fortunate

until you pivot
owning guarding

capsizing your small
spool of heat

then giddy
axe the day

tired of forgiving yourself for a
mosaic of privilege

sometimes you are so hot you
say yes to the cold

open a window
to let in the icy night air

and shiver a little
under your feather-down duvet

## Advice from an Alligator Pear

Forget about your book for now.

Instead, lift the lid off your compost bin and
amongst the eggshells and banana peels
find the discarded avocado pit.

This round unassuming wonder
will teach you everything you need to be a writer.
Which means time, more than anything.

You have always been too impatient.
Soak and peel the stone, wrap it in wet gauze.
You will need to put your seed in a dark place.

Then force yourself to let go and forget.
Stop thinking about it to the point of neglect.
You will break the new roots

if you keep checking and worrying it.
Trust that there is something growing in the dark,
that it is willing to live if you let it.

The wait will feel almost unbearably long
but eventually a small white root will emerge.
It is ready to be brought out into the light now.

Stick the root in water and again
wait for growth. You may change the water from time
to time if you must but it isn't necessary.

Surrender your wish to control.
Sometimes your seed will split, leaving you with a halfling
that might not survive. Sometimes it will bear twins.

Whatever tall leggy shoot will grow, it won't
look the way you expected it.

It will keep changing.

Have your scissors ready.
Don't forget to prune the top off regularly.
Teach yourself to be unsentimental

about those early leaves in whose
slow, slow, slow emergence
you were so invested.

All you have to do now is watch it grow,
and don't let it die.
Keep it alive. Keep it alive.

# frog

you are walking down the road
at night

out alone with
only a medium size poodle cross for protection

you're holding a filched branch of spring
blossoms in one hand

a bag with dog poo in the other
just wondering if there might be a poem in this

(the sweet blooming cherry
to bring a little of the scent of the season inside

offset by the stench of the dog shit
that is poking out of its half-torn little bag)

when you encounter the frog -
it springs suddenly from a dark corner

into your path and waits there
stares up at you with its uncanny eyes

and you start crying because
it is pure chance that this frog is a simple frog

that this frog is not a man with a knife to your throat
that you have to live in a world where

every night in another dark
corner of your sublime, stinking planet

another woman like you
was not quite as lucky

# Chapter Three

## A Spotter's Guide
## to Wings and Wonder

## Sleep Lessons From Birds

I.)
there are dates in the year
when the nights are so bright
even owls become larks

II.)
remember the kindness of sleep is winged
but claw-footed: sleep looks like an eagle-sized nightjar,
poised to swoop down where it spots you

III.)
in a nest, on a tree branch, a rooftop,
a trunk hole, mid-river, or down in the earth:
choose wisely

IV.)
dream of the sky,
dream of yourself as one stitch
in a murmuration

V.)
close your grip, let the tendons
in your talons tighten as you perch,
and you won't worry about falling

VI.)
watch out for the moths,
they steal tears while you sleep,
don't let them drink from your eyes

VII.)
if you ask the swifts you should
sleep on the wing, once
you are high enough to glide

## this is when

this is not just a picture
this a moment in time before it all -

it is a moment in time
it is a blue sky

ferns in the heat
at the height of their unfurling

this is the minute
before you ask the question

and I am forced to detonate my reply
into the quiet frenzy of greening

one two-
letter word

it feels worse
than just causing a fracture

it feels like dropping
an entire mountain

onto a near-extinct bird's only remaining
miniscule egg

## 22 02 2022

Ugh the clouds do mean business today.
Clearly I am not supposed to witness

a mere sunset:
this is epic theatre. Opera, even.

Set over the mythical rooftops and cupolas
of this ancient movie-set city,

a farewell is taking its torturously beautiful time,
like a key unlocking a mystery box.

Not subtle. In fact, everything about it is almost too much.
The spongy horizon folding in on itself,

the slant and slow bleeding out
of colour and light

from amber to dogwood to grey ice.
*Here's your message,* it belts out, *your omen, you dolt!*

*The word you have been looking for*
*in this unrepeatable aria of sky-wash and radiance is*

*Wonder. Wonder. Wonder.*

## Once There Were Willows

I sit where once
there were willows.
Once? Yesterday.
They came in their high-vis jackets

with chainsaws,
an electric shredder:
Fine men from
the council, hell-bent

on transforming
this green space forever.
I watched them suspiciously
from a distance

and so did the crows.
I think I am slowly becoming
one of their number, growing proficient
at flapping and perching and looking bedraggled.

Almost an expert already at making
mournful unanswered calls into the night.
We keep a record. We witness.
We use each other's words to recount

a disappearance of willows
so we will not forget.

## Eyrar

on your way to meet a stranger with a dead
phone in your pocket and your unpredictable
shadow in tow with its teeth and opinions you worry
about this impending encounter since your mind is nothing
if not a finely honed anxiety-machine

but as you cross onto the narrow bridgeway
that leads to the open meadow of the nature reserve
you spot her and smile
with the relief of recognition
because she looks just like her online picture

however there is something wrong
with her face
a strange halo of grief
as she gestures to keep you from approaching
you see it a second too late

something terrible to her left
a huge flap of white
streaked with red
it takes your brain
a moment to translate

the wrongness of these colours and shapes
you are seeing into a story
a swan has impaled himself
in two places
on the sharp metal fence

there is something about this scene
that you will never be able to unsee
to find pain where there should be beauty
to go from the moment of not-knowing
to a world that announces time is just code for sorrow

it is like the phone call that one year ago
turned all the people you have left into trapped injured birds
there is something about having to keep
your distance when your impulse is to come closer
to wait with the helpers

but this is a choice you will never be given
still the swan becomes a question binding you to the stranger
on the other side of the bridge and later a lady from the animal rescue
will call you both to let you know that he's eating
that he may make it through the night

## animal rescue

a small animal comes and
rescues me
every day

sometimes it is a puffed-up
sparrow seeking me
out in the garden

a bee coming to find me
to buzz importantly and dance
around my empty wine glass twice

a miniscule snail on my door
or a spider weaving
in the bathroom window

sometimes not even that small
a far-off falcon or a cow
holding my gaze in a field

sometimes an old dog puts her
soft head on my knee then sighs with her eyes
closed so that I too remember to breathe

sometimes not even an animal at all
just a cheerful shape in the sky
a half-remembered line

I thought I had no religion but perhaps
all of this is sacred
all I know is I am here

as if I had
allowed myself to be
returned

# taming a night mare in ten easy steps

I.

feeding the night mare
a diet of moth wings

the wick of a candle
a couple of hinges

a collection of thunder
and anguish

II.

calling the night mare
by the true name of the moon

in a language of
clockwords

III.

gentling the night mare with
strange laughter and board games

hours of shrieking
odd feathers

a joining of night air and a cloudscape
of shrinking and growing

VI.

teaching the night mare
a song with a swing door


V.

disguising the night mare
as a deer in a stairwell

a library of secrets
a swansong for milkmaids

a hoof-shaped house
a half-read book

on how to dream
in icelandic


VI.

storing the night mare
in a pocket of weather

between the lapwings
and nightjars

inside the architecture of an aging
queen's hair


VII.

washing the night mare in rumours of women
arriving on mars in a rocket

VIII.

riding the night mare
through an unruly city

past the favourite house
of a dream-faring stranger

through a small wisdom of newborns
towards the opposite of a tower


IX.

letting go of the night mare
in the dawn of a duvet

just before the streetlamps
get any ideas


X.

forgetting the night mare
like a poem or a password

a vague childhood sorrow a promise
or just the location

of a very important key
while constellations get restless

and time is unspooling
a skein of alarms

## Surgeon

*The heart surgeon is very very young. Maybe half as old as me. He looks like a mini version of the German TV host Thomas Gottschalk. His hair is in curly gold ringlets and his smile is too bright, his teeth their own luminous creatures. I am trying to work out why I am here with him. It must be that he is trying to operate on my heart in some way, make repairs. "There is nothing wrong with it!" I shout. "So you better put that knife down." "It's a scalpel," he says. Still, he does put it down, but also steps a little closer. Then he sighs, and shows me his calm hands. He's wearing marbled gloves. Then he reaches inside my chest and pulls something out with great gentleness. "There," he says. "See, that wasn't so bad." The thing he is holding out to me is a light blue egg, as big as a fist. I reach for it, but the shell is already opening, already releasing an infinite dark wing and another, unfolding like so many parachutes until everything is feather. I understand that it could never have hatched inside of me, there simply would not have been enough room. I look around for the Gottschalk child but he is no longer there: It's just me and the infinite bird.*

# I went out today looking for wonder

Found a wind,
two ducks.

Fifteen clouds shaped like
questions containing their own answer,

the way only water can
shapeshift itself.

I found a tree that had decided to start its spring early,
regardless of the general consensus.

I found a stick that had made
a dog's morning.

I found a well-rested sun with a six-hour workday
and a penchant for early nights.

Cycling back home on the towpath at nightfall,
I startled water rats.

The moon was a luminous fingernail
reflected below in the darkness to both sides of my wheels.

The flooding had turned the river
into a mirror, the meadows into a lake.

I wanted to show it to you,
each incredible marvel, and say:

*Look, oh, look,*
*see how the good world still holds you.*

# We Weren't Raised by Wolves But

the sea birds were our teachers
in matters of oil and drinking and running away

the forest birds had pointers
on how to have fights or make love on the glen

the pet birds let us know that
if the people in charge forget about you

you soon run out of water and die
so you must sing to survive

# Thank-Yous

First of all, my most heartfelt thanks to the fantastic, supportive super-woman of a publisher: Helen, I am so in awe of everything you do!

To the wonderful Rebecca Goss for selecting these poems for the Live Canon Collection Award and making a dream come true...

To the Arthur Welton Award by the Society of Authors for their absolutely invaluable financial support and encouragement.

To Terry Pratchett and his Librarian for preemptively shelving this book in the Unseen University Library long before it came into being.

Infinite gratitude to Rosie Caldecott for the amazing cover image and for everything, everything. (Everyone reading this, you need Rosie's art in your life. Trust me.)

Special shout-out to my parents Banu and Dietmar, my magical sisters Jessica and Waleska, my genius nephews Leo and Julius and my little niece Philippa who is my role model in everything.

To all my teachers and my writing heroes and crazy-talented inspiring writing friends. Léonie, Sophie, Jennie, Jess, Jak, Cesca, Clare, Harriet, Rowena, Robin, Maya, Jack, Daisy, Matt, Kiran, Tom, Sarvat, Lucy A., Sylee, Rachael, Juliane, Elodie, Paul, Rose, MK, JC, Allie, Sam, Calum, Ditte, Claire, Aget, Lucy D., Eva, Aurelie, Pia, Alev, Chris, Anders, Vicky, Klaus, Steffi, Fab, and Phoebe. The Catweazle Community, the Oxford Poetry Community, the Oxford Poetry Library, the Poetry and Pancakes Book Club, the LIT Poetry Group, the Storytellers' Supper Club.

To Sam D. for all the dog-sitting, and Dina and Hannah, for all the surprise treats.

To all the editors and competition judges who opened doors for my poems to sneak through.

To all the lovely people who bought my books or found my poems and got in touch about them, you have no idea how much your kindness has meant to me.

And finally, to Nick and Wodehouse for being the kindest man and silliest dog, respectively.

LIVE CANON